Dear Parents,

Children's earliest experiences with stories and books usually involve grown-ups reading to them. However, reading should be active, and as adults, we can help young readers make meaning of the text by prompting them to relate the book to what they already know and to their personal experiences. Our questions will lead them to move beyond the simple story and pictures and encourage them to think beneath the surface. For example, after reading a story about the sleep habits of animals, you might ask, "Do you remember when you moved into a big bed? Could you see the moon out of your window?"

Illustrations in these books are wonderful and can be used in a variety of ways. Your questions about them can direct the child to details and encourage him or her to think about what those details tell us about the story. You might ask the child to find three different "beds" used by animals and insects in the book. Illustrations can even be used to inspire readers to draw their own pictures related to the text.

At the end of each book, there are some suggested questions and activities related to the story. These questions range in difficulty and will help you move young readers from the text itself to thinking skills such as comparing and contrasting, predicting, applying what they learned to new situations and identifying things they want to find out more about. This conversation about their reading may even result in the children becoming the storytellers, rather than simply the listeners!

Harriet Ziefert, M.A.
Language Arts/Reading Specialist

More to  About

Does a Woodpecker Use a Hammer?

Does a Bear Wear Boots?

Does a Beaver Sleep in a Bed?

Does a Camel Cook Spaghetti?

Does an Owl Wear Eyeglasses?

Does a Tiger Go to the Dentist?

Doe a Hippo Go to the Doctor?

Does a Seal Smile?

Think About how everyone learns

Does a Panda Go to School?

Harriet Ziefert • illustrations by **Emily Bolam**

BLUE APPLE

Text copyright © 2003, 2014 by Harriet Ziefert
Illustrations copyright © 2003 by Emily Bolam
All rights reserved
CIP data is available.
Published in the United States 2014 by
🍎 Blue Apple Books
South Orange, New Jersey

Who goes to school?
Does a panda?

Don't be silly! A panda doesn't go to school.

A panda prefers to be alone and would not really enjoy making new friends.

Does an ostrich go to school?

No, an ostrich could not follow directions from the teacher.

An ostrich could not put his jacket and backpack in a cubby.

Does an armadillo go to school?
No way!

An armadillo could not do arithmetic.

Or sit still and listen to a story!

A chimpanzee is smart—smarter than a panda, an ostrich, or an armadillo.

Could a chimp go to school?

A chimp likes to be with others.
It might have fun with children.

A chimp could paint a picture.

A chimp could learn to use a computer.

But a chimp couldn't sing!

Or read a book!

Or learn to share!

A chimp "speaks" by making sounds.
When a scientist spends a lot of time with one,
he can understand what the chimp is saying.

"Wah Wah!"
But a chimp cannot talk with words.

A chimp cannot ask to be excused to go to the bathroom.

A chimp would like snack time.
But he might throw
banana peels on the floor!

A chimp would be excellent on the playground.

A chimp could not tell his mom about what he did in school when she came to pick him up.

**And he could not say to his friends,
"Bye, see you all tomorrow."**

Think  About how everyone learns

This book compares what a panda, an ostrich, an armadillo, and a chimp could learn in school to what a child could learn.

Compare and Contrast

For the most part, people are the only animals who go to school. Compare what a dog can learn at dog school to what you learn at your school:

- List 10 things a dog can learn.
- List 10 things you can learn.

A chimp could do some things you do at school, but not everything.

- What are some things you can do that a chimp can't do?
- What are some things a chimp can do that you can't do?
- What are the things you and a chimp both can do?

If animals don't go to school, what do they do all day?

- What does a lion do? A robin?
- What does a bumblebee do? A fish?

Research

Animals have been taught to do amazing things by people. Go to a library or online and find out:

- What have chimps, dolphins, and horses been taught to do?

Some dogs go to obedience school.

- What kinds of things do dogs learn at these schools?
- How do their teachers train them?

Observe

Watch a toddler play with toys for 15 minutes.

- What did the toddler learn?
- What did the toddler practice?

Watch a pet and see what it knows about the people and places in its home.

- Make a list of the things it knows about eating, sleeping, getting attention, or going outside.

Watch an animal in your neighborhood.

- What are some things it can do that you can do?
- What are some things it can do that you would like to be able to do?

Write, Tell, or Draw

Write, or tell, a story about:

- What I Learned in School Today
- What I Didn't Learn in School Today

What kind of animal would you like to bring to school?

- Write, tell, or draw how the animal would change the school day.

What if chimps went to "chimp school" and you got to go, too?

- Write about what it would be like in "chimp school" and what you might learn.
- Draw what a chimp school would look like.

www.ingramcontent.com/pod-product-compliance
Lightning Source LLC
LaVergne TN
LVHW070837080426
835510LV00026B/3425